Conqueror

A Daily Devotional

Breaking Chains of PTSD

One Link at a Time

One Lie at a Time

By: Tabytha L. Wynn

ISBN:9780578279220

Editor: Your Book Journey Consulting, LLC

Dedication

This book is dedicated to my husband, Mark, the biggest conqueror I know, my children whom I love with all my heart, everyone who reads this book and finds healing, and above all, my Lord and Savior, Jesus Christ.

Contents

Thank You

Adoptive Family- Words cannot express how much you all have meant to me. Since I was eight years old, your home has been a safe and loving place for me to go. Thank you for showing me the love of Christ by accepting me into your family. Thank you, Dad, for showing me the example of a loving father. Without that, I don't think I would have understood the love of Christ. Thank you, Mom, for loving me and showing me how to be a loving mother to my children. Special thanks to my dear sisters, to whom I've grown closer these last few years. Your love means more than you could ever know.

Bobby Joe- Thank you for teaching me to live radically for Christ and showing me that I am more than a conqueror in Christ.

Bridge Family- Thank you for your love and prayers over the years. You guys will always be our family! There might be a distance in miles, but we will always be together through God's love. Thank you for always being our family.

Celebrate Recovery Family- Thank you for giving me a safe place to recover and grow in Christ. I am entirely grateful for everything you have done for my family and me.

Don and Grace- Thank you for all your kindness and support since we moved in. I am grateful for your patience as I have healed.

Eddie and Tammy- Thank you for everything you've done over the years. I wouldn't be who I am today if you hadn't taken me in as your own. Thank you for all the love you've shown me. Thank you for being there for my family and me. Thank you for adopting me in your heart.

Ellan- Thank you for your continued love and support since I was a child. Sometimes your phone calls were the only thing getting me through the week.

Gateway Church Family – Thank you for showing me the love of a Christ-centered church family and that such a family exists. Thank you for all you've done for my family and me. Without the love and support of all of you, my recovery wouldn't have been possible.

Kent and Joy- Thank you for loving Mark and me at our worst because you saw the best in us and for seeing what Jesus could accomplish in our lives.

Lee and Tina- Thank you for showing me Jesus and the truth of the Gospel. Thank you for being there for me for so many years. God has used you in so many ways over the years. I could never list them all.

Mickey- Thank you for being a great friend and brother in Christ all these years; thank you, especially for stopping what you were doing and praying with me.

Pastor Ray- I thank you for giving me and my family someplace safe to worship and grow in our walk with God. Thank you for your honesty and ability to preach the Word of God without fear and for the unconditional love and support you have shown us.

Why I Wrote This Book

When I felt called to write this book, my conversation with God went like this.

Me: God, I know you know better than me, but I'm still struggling with PTSD. I'm feeling weighed down by my past hurts and poor choices. How can I tell others they are more than conquerors when I don't feel like a conqueror?

God: That's why you should write it because you are where they are.

Me: But- (insert more excuses here).

God: Will you obey my calling in your life or not?

Me: Ouch

I've walked around defeated so much that I forgot whose I am and what I can do if I'm willing to trust in Him and follow His steps. I felt defeated, discouraged, overwhelmed, depressed, hopeless, helpless, and unable to rise above the foolish choices I made while my trauma controlled me. I have also faced some of the things you are facing right now. I still struggle some days, but overall, God has healed my trauma. A great deal of my healing came from writing this book. You see, as I dove more and more into the lie-defeating truth of His Word, I was more healed. A great deal of this book is made up of notes from my healing journey, re-written for you. As I wrote my notes in book form, God began healing me even more. So, know, dear brothers and sisters, as you read my words, many of them were written from a place where you find yourself. Instead of staying in that place of darkness, decide that you are not defeated and rise up a Conqueror.

How To Use This Book

This devotional was written to help you replace the lies you believe with God's truth. God's truth can only be found in His Word, the Bible. This devotional was not written to be used as a substitution for scripture, nor was it written to add to scripture. This book was created to be a stepping stone into the scriptures. Those who struggle with PTSD or other mental health issues tend to work harder to complete everyday tasks and feel overwhelmed with caring for the needs of themselves and others. Therefore, picking up the Bible (a large piece of literature) can feel overwhelming. Nonetheless, the Bible is where the healing begins; in its pages, we find the truth of God's love and the power of His healing over our lives. The Bible is where we find the One we can turn our lives, hearts, struggles, faults, hurts, and sins over to....Jesus Christ. This is where true healing begins.

When an event or a season of life leads you to develop PTSD, the issues are more than just flashbacks and nightmares; in fact, it completely takes over your mind. This is especially true for those who survived abuse and those involved in combat. The lies creep in little by little, quickly taking over the way you think and distort your mind. For example, thinking "I'm useless" after a childhood of being beaten and called useless, or being overwhelmed by guilt after surviving time in the military or police force, etc. I don't have combat history personally, so my perspective in this book will be that of a survivor of many forms of abuse, mainly as a child. I want to share the freedom I found in the truth about God and His thoughts toward me. I know how easy it is to believe Satan's lies in your mind and how hard it can be to find the truth. I know what it's like to doubt God and His love for us. This is the reason I wrote this book! It wasn't until I got into His words that I learned the truth and started defeating those lies. I pray that reading this book every day will enable you to begin to break chains, dive deeper into His Word, and learn about the only One who truly sets us free, Jesus Christ.

This book is a devotional; it's not a bible study. I won't be getting into every point about every piece of scripture, although I would love to. Instead, I will share some scripture portions and what we can learn about God's truth from the text. This book includes twenty-three "Lies" and nine "Truth Points." You can choose to read one lie or truth point in order, OR you can go to the contents and pick which lies you would like to read first if you have a lie that seems extra heavy at that moment. Please DO NOT read the book all at once; instead, take some time to read a lie or a truth point a day and devote that time to God and you're healing.

PLEASE seek help from family, friends, doctors, therapists, pastors, or a mental health professional. PTSD is a battle not won by fighting alone! This is especially true for those who struggle with depression and suicidal thoughts. Seeking God is where the healing comes from; often, He uses professionals and medication to aid in that healing. YOU ARE NOT any less of a Christian for taking medication and seeking professional help. If you had a broken leg, would you pray and wait for a miracle, OR would you pray and then go to the ER? Now that we got that out let's continue our journey by looking at the layout and sections I've designed to aid your journey.

<u>Lies #1-23</u>

Lie #: A lie we often believe.

Truth: The truth found in God's Word that defeats the lie.

Scripture: A passage in the Bible to discover the truth.

Devotional Text: A short story with an explanation of the text and how it can be applied.

Write About It: A writing prompt to encourage deeper thinking on the subject.

Prayer: A prayer to God about the topic.

Memory Verse: A short verse from the passage to commit to memory.

Song Suggestions: A song that goes with the devotional. If you don't have a way of looking up the song suggestion, DO NOT worry. This is only a bonus for you.

Truth Points #1-9

Truth Points contain stories, things I learned in my own life, and scripture. A few of them have been written by other men and women of God. Truth points are designed to give you more insights and perspectives as you walk the journey of healing with Jesus.

Introduction

We, as Christians, underestimate Satan's power over our minds. Because we tend to overly focus on the heart, we don't consider the mind or believe that the mind isn't a factor even after it's considered. Please understand me. I believe the condition of the heart is essential; in fact, the Bible is very clear about the heart and its importance in our lives. A few examples can be found in 1 Samuel 16:7, Matthew 5:21-28, and Luke 6:45. However, the battle of the heart first begins in our minds. We must not ignore the spiritual battle that rages on in our minds if we are going to guard our hearts and have a heart that lives for Christ. The battle often begins with a few sneaky words or phrases that sound right but are Satan's sly way of beginning to twist things around. Twisting things can lead us to believe lies about God, His thoughts toward us, and what we think about ourselves. This is especially true for those battling mental health issues such as PTSD, anxiety, and depression. We can see the first example of a psychological attack when we read the account between Satan and Eve in Genesis.

Picture it. There was Eve in paradise with a loving God, her husband, animals, all the food she could ever want, and splendor around her. The only rule was "DO NOT eat the fruit of a certain tree." That's it! Not hard, right? I imagine Eve thought the same thing and was perfectly happy with this arrangement. That is until Satan enters the picture as a serpent. Most have probably read or heard this passage before but let's look closer at the tricks he plays on her mind.

'Now the serpent was more cunning than any beast of the field which the Lord had made, and he said to the woman. Has God, indeed, said you shall not eat of every tree of the garden?' Notice the two things he did. The first thing to notice is that he called The Lord God "God." If you read the first two chapters in Genesis, you will see that God is referred to as THE LORD GOD. Satan refers to Him as just GOD. He did not acknowledge that God was Lord; thus, he subtly put the idea in her mind that God was not Lord of her life but rather just someone in her life. He introduces the idea that God isn't the Lord over all creation, just someone in creation. Second, notice he asked her a question. He didn't just say, "Hey, don't trust God. Go eat some fruit." Instead, he put this question in her mind, "What did God really say?"

Let's read on. Genesis 3:2-6, "And the woman said to the serpent, 'We may eat the fruit of the trees of the garden, but of the fruit of the tree which is in the midst of the garden, God has said, 'You shall not eat it. Nor shall you touch it, lest you die.' And the serpent said to the woman, 'You will not surely die for God knows that in the day you eat of it, your eyes will be open, and you will be like God, knowing good and evil.' So when the woman saw that the tree was good for food, that it was pleasant to the eyes, and the tree desirable to make one wise, she took of its fruit, and she also gave her husband with her, and he ate."

Don't miss this! Satan was able to convince Eve that God was lying to her. Satan caused Eve to question God and His love for her and doubt her trust in Him. Satan was able to convince Eve to trust his word over the Word of the Lord of all creation. He accomplished this while Eve was living in paradise, a non-fallen world. God had given her more than we could imagine in our wildest imaginations and didn't ask much of her in return. Yet, she was so easily convinced to betray God. He did it to her then, and he does it to us now. If Satan can trick Eve, then how much easier is it for Satan to deceive us here in a fallen world? A world full of chaos, destruction, pain, death, and even everyday distractions of life. I assure you, if he could get inside Eve's mind in paradise, surely, he can get into our minds here. We must guard our hearts and minds with God's truth. God's Word is the only power we have over the lies Satan inputs into our minds. Just as Eve had the choice to listen to Satan, so do we. We must choose the truth over lies. We must learn God's truth to be set free from Satan's lies.

For those of us who battle mental health and PTSD, we are especially at risk of choosing Satan's lies over God's truths. Some of us fall prey to the abuse and words our abusers have ingrained in us, lies that we have believed to be true about ourselves and God, which is the biggest tragedy. Abuse can leave us with the belief that God doesn't really love us or that His love must be earned. I say "we, ourselves, and us" because I want you to know you are not alone. There are so many of us who struggle with PTSD and believe so many lies. I struggled with PTSD, mental health issues, and even a brain injury for years, but God! God put the right people and treatments in my life to show me the truth about God, His love, and myself. Although I still have my bad days, even in those days, I am a conqueror in Christ Jesus. Praise God! Many men, women, brothers, and sisters in Christ are struggling; our feelings and stories may differ, but the battles are similar. Do you feel that way? Are you feeling weighed down by past abuse or mistakes? Are you struggling to grow closer to God? Maybe getting up out of bed every day is a daunting task. Today, brothers and sisters, as you begin this book, you begin the journey to breaking the chains of PTSD. One link in the chain at a time. One lie at a time.

Lie#1: I'm a damaged, defeated victim.
Truth: In Christ, we are more than conquerors.

Read: Romans 8:31-39

I used to walk around defeated because I was convinced that the lies I believed were true. Lies like: "You will never be good enough." "You will never rise above this situation." "You will never forget what happened to you." "You will never be able to move on." "You will never be able to let go." "You are nothing more than a damaged, defeated victim." These lies and false belief systems did not appear in one day. It started with a little lie I believed about myself, a lie that was put on me by my abuser, and it grew. Lies are like that; they don't seem like a big deal at first; maybe it's just a little false belief or an old wives' tale, perhaps something that's not entirely accurate, but then it grows into a bigger problem until it becomes life-threatening. It is easy for someone to slip into a dark place that resorts to horrific consequences. Committing suicide is one possibility, as well as self-harm and eating disorders, to name a few more. Do you see how lies can grow into a bigger problem if not dealt with? We can quickly go from being children of the Most High God and feeling and living as such to walking around defeated. Think of the majestic horse. Horses are so powerful and magnificent, but one small thing can become life-threatening to a horse; a broken leg. It is often a death sentence. A fractured leg heals on most living creatures, but to your horse, it usually means the end. Just as a broken leg can mean the end to a horse, so can lies be to us. I urge you, don't take the lies that you are a damaged victim lightly. You do not have to walk around as if you are defeated.

Romans 8:31 -37 tells us that we are more than conquerors in Christ Jesus, who died for us. We do not have to fear our enemies; we do not have to wonder what happens to us next. No one can defeat us, not if we trust in God. We know that God will always be there because He gave His son for us, even when we were His enemies. If He didn't withhold His son from us while we were still His enemies, what would He withhold from His children? Nothing! Therefore, we can confidently know that He is fighting with us and for us and that nothing can separate us from the love of God and the plans He has for us. Nothing! No matter the struggle or hurt, we, in Christ, are more than conquerors. Yes, you are a conqueror over your history, abuse, and PTSD.

Write About It: "I am more than a conquer because JESUS fights with me!" What do those words mean to you? How are you still walking as a defeated victim?

Prayer: Lord, help me remember that no matter what has happened in my life, both in the past and present, in you, I am more than a conqueror. Lord, walk beside me as I fight my battle to overcome my challenges with PTSD. Help me to know that nothing can separate me from your love. In Jesus' name, Amen.

Memory Verse: Romans 8:37- *Yet in all these things, we are more than conquerors through Him who loved us.*

Song Suggestion: "More Than Conquerors" -Steven Curtis Chapman

Lie #2: I'm worthless.
Truth: I have value because the King of all creation has chosen me to be His child from the beginning of time.

Read: Ephesians 1:3-12

Imagine for a moment a father receiving a notice that his child has been kidnapped. His child is trapped in the darkness, somewhere lost. The only way the father can get his child back is by giving up all he has to pay the ransom for his child. So, of course, he gives all he holds dear to free his child and bring that child back to himself. Why? Because he loves his child, his child is valuable to him.

Like the father in our story, brothers and sisters, God sent His precious son to pay our ransom. A paid ransom that would be our rescue from the darkness and bring us back to Him. He sent His only son out of his home in Heaven, down to Earth, to live a sinless life and then suffer and die. The incredible thing about this is that this was in God's plan from the very beginning before He created us; before he made anything, he knew we would fail. He knew we would rebel against Him. He knew He would have to send Jesus, and He knew Jesus would sacrifice Himself and give Himself up for us. He knew, and yet He chose us anyway. He chose a plan for us to bring us out of darkness and into His light and adopted us as one of His children. Brothers and sisters, you have value. We have value. God wouldn't have chosen that plan for us if He didn't value us. Jesus wouldn't have paid the ransom for us if he didn't love us. Verse 12, Ephesians chapter 1 tells us we receive this adoption by the blood of Jesus, referring to His death on the cross and us putting our trust in Him. We will address "Trusting in Jesus" more in the coming days, but I urge you, if you cannot yet count yourself as a brother or sister in Christ or if you have doubts, let today be the day that you decide to trust in Him.

Write About It: "I am a child of God! I have value because I am loved and chosen by Him" What do these words mean to you? Do you believe them?

Prayer: Lord, I praise You for who You are. Thank You for choosing me. Thank You for sending Your son to die so I can be Yours. Please help me remember that I have value and am not worthless because I am your child. Amen.

Memory Verse: Ephesians 1:4 - *just as He chose us in Him before the foundation of the world, that we should be holy and without blame before Him in love.*

Song Suggestion: "Hello, My Name Is" -Matthew West

Lie#3 I can't go to God; He's too angry at me. Truth: God is your father who will never stop loving you no matter what you have done.

Read: Luke 15:11-22

As an adult, I was adopted after several attempts to reconcile with my biological parents. I was adopted by a family who had been there to support me throughout my childhood and early adulthood. I always felt safe at their home, and they always made me feel welcome. My dad has been one of the only father figures who hasn't abused me. He has shown me nothing but Jesus' love. Guess what, though? I still wonder, "Does he regret adopting me?" "If I tell him the stupid thing I just did, will he stop loving me?" What has my dad done that gives me this idea? NOTHING! He's never done anything but support and loves my family and me. I remember one time I went to him about something I messed up on, you know, again, and he lovingly gave me advice and solutions, you know, again. Afterward, I offered to take out his trash for him. I was going to the dump anyways, and my dad, with all the love in his heart, kept asking, "Are you sure? It's no problem, is it? Well, thanks so much!" as if I offered him a million dollars. After I left, I just cried; after everything I'd done wrong, his love was unconditional. He didn't say, "Yeah, you better take out the trash after coming to me with another problem" NO! He was happy that his daughter thought of him. I remember thinking, "Boy, he doesn't deserve the thoughts I think about his love being conditional, does he?" Then the Lord spoke to my heart and said, "I don't either." That's the moment I realized that I never really trusted God as my father, and I began to open my heart.

My thoughts about my dad and God didn't come from anything they did to me. These thoughts came from years of being abused by other father figures. It came from years of being taught that love was conditional. Is that true for you? Are you afraid to go to God because you've messed up too much, or you're afraid you can't trust Him? Jesus told the parable in Luke 15:11-22 as an example of the Father's love for us. The father in the story didn't show anger toward him. Instead, he ran to his son and greeted him with loving arms. Our heavenly father is the same way; He chases after us. Run into His loving, open arms because He loves you.

Write About It: How do you feel towards your heavenly father? Do you know that you can run to Him and that His arms are open to you?

Prayer: Thank You, Lord, for loving us and forgiving us. No matter what any of us have done, Father God, You welcome us with open arms as one of Your children. Help me, Father, to trust You and run to You. Thank You for Your forgiveness. -Amen

Memory Verse: Luke 15:24 - *for this my son was dead and is alive again; he was lost and is found.' And they begin to be merry.*

Song suggestion: "Run to the Father" - Matt Maher

Lie#4: God's going to punish me.
Truth: We are covered by the blood of Christ.

Read: 1 John 4:17-19

Fear of God's judgment was always a struggle for me. I would think things like, "Has God really forgiven me? Is there a 'step' I'm missing? Jesus' blood can't cover everything, can it? There must be more that I need to do. It can't be that simple. As soon as I die, I'm going to discover that there are things I didn't do because God's still angry at me about something, and all His wrath will come down on me." Have you had this way of thinking? I had this way of thinking due to the harsh judgment and punishments I received from people who had authority over me. Perhaps the same is true for you as well. It's a common issue in those struggling with PTSD from abuse by parents and other authority figures. However, we can know this way of thinking is a lie because of what today's Bible passage tells us.

1 John 4 tells us that we can stand before God with BOLDNESS. No dread, no fear, no regrets, but boldness. Where does this boldness or confidence come from? Jesus. Jesus' blood covers all our sins! When we stand before God, that's all He sees. Picture for a minute being at a fancy party. Only the rich and famous are allowed to attend. Picture yourself as the town homeless person, and you are confronted by security and the party's host! What would you do? Just before they kick you out, they notice who is standing next to you. The son of the host! Oh yeah, that's right. He invited you; YOU are his plus one! So, you look over at the security and host and say, "I'm with him." Being with him is your free ticket to the party, just as you are. You are Jesus'

"plus one." You are welcomed by His blood. Nothing we could do or say could make us clean or worthy. Go to God with the confidence that you are His. You can go to God with confidence because Jesus paid "your ticket" already. You can go fearless because His perfect love casts out fear, the perfect love that He showed by dying on the cross. There is no fear in love; fear is a lie from the enemy. You are with Jesus; there are no other requirements.

Write About It: What are some reasons why you think God will judge you? How do you know those things are covered?

Prayer: Dear Father, I thank You for Jesus's sacrifice. I ask forgiveness for those times when I thought that the sacrifice Jesus made was not good enough and I was afraid of Your judgment. Lord, I invite You to take these worries away and remind me daily that God keeps no record of my wrongs. Amen.

Memory verse: 1 John 4:18a - *There is no fear in love, but perfect love casts out fear.*

Song Suggestion: "Perfect Love"- Austin French

Lie #5: I’m useless.
Truth: God has a plan and purpose for me, even if others can’t see it.

Read: 1 Samuel 17:20-37

Unfortunately, I have believed the lie “I’m useless” since childhood. It was first conceived by my abusers calling me names and putting me down with every failure, but it was kept alive by the harsh words of those around me. In some cases, I made the mistake of villainizing people who spoke harshly toward me. Although there are cases in which people have an agenda or malicious intent, some say harsh things but have the best intentions. So, I'm learning that when things are said in the wrong way or at the wrong time to be careful not to assume they mean harm to me. It’s essential to be mindful of those who only love you and want what’s best for you and your situation. This can be challenging because even if the things people say are from a place of love, the wrong tone can cause distrust and discouragement and even cause you to doubt God’s plan and purpose. Thus, leading you to question your usefulness.

David's father, Jesse, sent him to the battlefield to take supplies to his brothers. David left his sheep with "a keeper" and met up with his brothers. When David arrived at the battlefield, he saw the Israelite warriors standing around, trying to figure out what to do about the giant Philistine, Goliath. David spoke up about this to the warriors and even went to Saul to say that he would fight Goliath. David’s brother, Eliab, was angry at David for what he was saying to the warriors about the battle and the fact that he had left the sheep.

King Saul told David he wasn't strong enough to defeat the giant. Now, Eliab and Saul weren't necessarily wrong for thinking the way they did or talking the way they did to David. They may have been trying to guide David in the right direction; they may have had David's best interest at heart. The Bible isn't clear on their intentions; however, it's reasonable to believe they weren't totally in the wrong because David would have been speaking out of term and against the traditions of that time. What's important here isn't what was said to David but David's response. After talking to his brother and the king, David didn't say, "Well, I guess they are right. I'm better off just going back to my sheep." Instead, he said, "God will deliver me from the hands of the Philistine (the giant)." Even after being discouraged, David went to battle anyway. Therefore brothers and sisters, instead of allowing people's harsh words to lead you to believe you are useless, choose to believe what God's telling you and go to battle anyway.

Write About It: What are some words from your abuser or words from those around you that have led you to believe you are useless? What are some things that you CAN do well? How can you use these things for God?

Prayer: Dear Father, thank You for creating me and having a plan for my life. I ask forgiveness for believing the enemy's lies and not what You say about me. Give me the strength and determination to follow You wherever You lead. In Jesus' name, I pray, Amen.

Memory Verse: 1 Samuel 17:37 - *Moreover, David said, "The LORD, who delivered me from the paw of the lion and from the paw of the bear, He will deliver me from the hand of this Philistine."*

Song Suggestion: "Good Fight" - Unspoken

Lie #6: I'm nothing.
Truth: God turns nothing into something.

Read: Genesis 1:1-13

"I'm nothing," "There's nothing good about me," "I'm just wasted space." These are just a few self-deprecating things I have said to myself. I've felt trapped in a dark emptiness, void of everything but anxiety and fear. But I assure you darkness and nothingness are God's specialty.

Looking at today's passage in Genesis, we see that the earth was empty and void, and darkness covered the whole world. So, God was there over the earth and said, "Let there be light," and there was light. At that very moment, there was light. He then went on to create everything else in the world. He took the chaos of nothingness and darkness and created everything. He created land, oceans, plants, animals, and of course, Adam and Eve. However, don't miss this! What was the very first thing He created in the empty world? Light! Then He did what? He separated the light from the darkness. After He created the earth, one of God's first divine commands was to bring order to the chaos by creating light and separating it from the darkness. When He spoke, the light entered, and the darkness fled immediately! That's where transformation starts by first separating the light from the darkness. That's where the transformation begins in your situation by bringing light to it. I'm speaking of the other light God sent us, His son, Jesus Christ. Jesus is a light. When He enters any situation, the darkness must flee.

I say to you today, let there be light! Let the darkness flee! Let there be light in the chaos, let there be light in every dark corner of your mind, and let there be light in your nothingness! You are not nothing! No matter what you are thinking or feeling, God can transform your situation and your struggle into something. Therefore, let there be light on your situation! Let the shining light of Jesus Christ and God's truth be that light. Accept His light into your nothingness.

Write About It: These negative narratives, like "I'm nothing," that the enemy tries to get us to believe are lies. We can no longer walk around in darkness because our Father sent Jesus to be the light in our situation. What are some negative narratives that come into your mind? What were you doing at the time they entered your mind?

Prayer: Father, I thank You for being that light in the darkness. Forgive me for believing those negative narratives and acting upon them. I realize now that You are the Light in my dark situations, and I need to believe only what You say about me and not what others say about me. In the name of Jesus, I pray, Amen.

Memory Verse: Genesis 1:3 - *Then God said, "Let there be light,"; and there was light.*

Song Suggestion: "Here for a Reason"- Ashes Remain

Lie #7: I'm too weak.
Truth: Don't use weakness as an excuse to stay where you are.

Read: John 5:3-8

This passage in John tells us that there was a pool, and around this pool were people that were sick, lame, blind, and had other various types of afflictions. They were waiting around the pool because, on certain days, angels would come and stir the pool. When this happened, the first person to get into the pool would be healed. At the pool, there was a man with an infirmity. Jesus asked him, "Do you want to be healed?" When Jesus asked him this, he replied that he couldn't get to the pool in time to be healed. So Jesus said to him, "Rise, take your bed and walk." The man was immediately healed, took his bed, and walked away.

The man at the pool had an infirmity which means weakness or powerlessness. He was weak and powerless, sitting by a pool. I wonder if he gave up. I wonder if he'd gotten so used to being weak and powerless that he didn't even care if he was healed. Notice Jesus asked him if he wanted to be healed. He had to want to be healed. You may have been stuck in the PTSD rut for so long that you've given up and just decided to stay where you are. Notice that Jesus not only asked him if he wanted to be healed, but he also gave him something to do, rise! Maybe you need to choose to rise up! If your PTSD is so bad you can't get out of bed, I say to you, in the name of Jesus, rise! Don't make excuses to stay where you are.

The man at the pool said that no one would help him to the pool in time to be healed; it sounds like an excuse to stay stuck, as if he had just given up even trying because no one would help him. When Jesus told him to rise, take his bed and walk, Jesus gave him a choice to stay where he was or accept the healing. We need to be careful not to use our weaknesses as an excuse to stay stuck. Although trauma can, and often does, leave us with lifelong issues leading us to feel weak and powerless, we need not use it as an excuse to stay stuck in a PTSD rut. We must choose to accept God's healing power in our lives. Let Jesus heal you. He won't work without your permission. You have to want it. You have to choose to stay where you are or rise up and walk. Allow Jesus to speak healing into your weakness.

Write About It: What areas are keeping you down or stuck where you are? Are you able to surrender those things to God?

Prayer: Lord, help me trust in You to heal me. Please help me to choose to rise up and walk instead of staying where I am. Thank You for being a healer in my life. Amen.

Memory Verse: John 5:8 - *Jesus said to him, "Rise, take up your bed and walk."*
Song Suggestion: "Healing"- Blanca

Lie #8: I can't---- until God----.
Truth: God's strength is made perfect in your weakness.

Read: 2 Corinthians 12:7-10

I have a traumatic brain injury, autism spectrum disorder, PTSD, and a past full of trauma and abuse. But I've seen God work in my life. For example, I struggle with reading, writing, and grammar, yet God is working on me through writing this book. I struggle with memory and connecting deeply with people, even my husband and children. I struggle with sensory overload, insecurity, anxiety, and just general issues with communicating with people and yet God. Yet, God had me standing up, reciting the books and sections of the Old Testament in front of my church on a Wednesday night. Yet, God had me giving a lesson in front of my Celebrate Recovery group. In fact, I've given a lesson quite a few times, and I continue to get better at it. I can't take credit for those things, though. It's all God! God gets the glory because there's no way I can do it on my own. I spent years asking God to remove my disorders from me, but God has said to me, "It's not about you; it's about Me. It's not by your strength but Mine. My grace is sufficient for you. My strength is made perfect in your weakness." God uses our weaknesses and brokenness for His glory!

In 2 Corinthians 12, Paul cried to God to remove the pain from him, but God told him, "My grace is sufficient for you. My strength is made perfect in weakness." How did Paul respond? Paul responded that he was going to be content in all things, good or bad, because, in his weakness, God was strong in his life. He was indispensable because of the power of Christ showing through him. If Paul didn't have this thorn on his side, he might have thought that everything God did through him was actually because of his power and not the incredible power of God. By leaving the thorn in his side, God was doing two things: He was showing Paul that he needed to lean on God for strength, not his own. Secondly, God put Paul in a position where he couldn't succeed without God. Therefore, God got the glory and the credit, not Paul. You might be crying out to God, asking Him to make you better or to remove something painful in your life right now. He might be saying no or not right now. You may, at this very moment, be feeling helpless. You may feel like you can't even get out of bed but remember, dear brother or sister, God can use you right there where you are, as you are. So, cry out to Him and remember that, in your weakness, He is strong.

Write About It: What are some of your weaknesses that you feel get in the way of being used by God? How could these weaknesses be strengths?

Prayer: God, thank You for using me, especially when I'm at my weakest. Help me trust in You and lean on You, not my strength or understanding. Amen.

Memory Verse: 2 Corinthians 12:9 - *And He said to me, "my grace is sufficient for you for my strength is made perfect in weakness."*

Song suggestions: "Walk by Faith" - Jeremy Camp, "In Me"- Casting Crowns

Lie #9: I can't --- because ---.
Truth: God's power gives you the power over your can't.

Read: Exodus 3:11-14 and 4:10-17

I'm not qualified to write this book. When my editor reads this, she might gasp at that statement and the fact that I would even consider telling my readers that I'm not qualified to write. However, it's the truth. I am not qualified. I indeed have experience with PTSD, and Jesus has transformed my mental health with the gospel's truth; those are the only qualifications I have. My reading and writing, and grammar skills are lacking; however, as it turns out, Jesus is the only qualification that I genuinely need.

In today's passage, Moses had fled Egypt after killing a man and had established a new life in the desert when one day, while tending his flock, God appeared to Moses and told him to go and free the people in Egypt. Moses wasn't qualified. He even told God he wasn't; he was a murderer, hadn't lived in Egypt for many years, and had some speech impairment or didn't see himself as gifted in speech. Moses asked, "God, who am I to go to speak to the pharaoh? Why are you sending me and not someone with more talent?" But God answered him by saying that He is the one that opens the mouth, the eyes, and the ears; he will go with Moses, and He will send someone to go with him. Moses felt inadequate and unqualified, and the truth is, he was.

But it wasn't about what Moses could or couldn't do. It was about what God could do. It was about God's power alone. God calls us to be His hands, feet, and mouthpiece. You may feel things are out of control, but don't worry because God is in control! Let God use your past and your trauma for His good! Give Him everything that's messed up! Give God the very thing that's weighing you down because He will use it to lift you up.

Write About It: What are the areas in your life where you feel inadequate? Has God revealed what He has called you to do despite your limitations? If so, what has He called you to do?

Prayer: God, show me what You are calling me to do even though I have limitations and feel inadequate. Please help me to trust You, Father, instead of my abilities. Amen.

Memory Verse: Exodus 4:12- *Now, therefore, go, and I will be with your mouth and teach you what you shall say.*

Song Suggestions: "Nobody"- Casting Crowns, "Christ In Me"- Jeremy Camp

Lie #10: God doesn't have a purpose for me. Truth: God had a plan and purpose for you before you were born.

Read: Jeremiah 1:4-9

"You have no purpose other than pleasing your man and cleaning!" That was the message I got from my biological father growing up; this is what I was taught about the role of women. As time passed, I believed I wasn't good enough for even those minimal views of women. At that time, I couldn't see my future; married with eight kids, an author, and a minister to other women. I couldn't have imagined it, but God had it planned before I was conceived.

The Lord spoke to Jeremiah and told him that not only was he called to be a prophet, but God had called him before he was growing inside his mother's womb. God set him apart from others in his nation to be a prophet with a specific agenda and purpose. The purpose God had was meant for him and only for him. But his response to the Lord was, "I'm too young." We do that to God, too, don't we? When God first called me to write, I told God I couldn't because----. Because there are eight kids in my house. Because I have this disability. Because I can't write well. Because I'm not the right person. When we and others around us often say we are the wrong person, God says, "You are just the right person." What did God say to Jeremiah after he said, "I can't"? God said to him, "Don't be ashamed. I will go to all I send you to. Don't be afraid of them; I will deliver you. I will give you the words to speak!" Guess what? The Lord touched his mouth and gave His words to Jeremiah! Just as He did that for Jeremiah, He's doing that in me. He's giving me the words to write, and if you are called to write, He can do that for you, too. He will guide you no matter what you're called to do.

It's not about what you can or cannot do, only what God can do. He will make a way even when there seems to be no way. He will use you for His purpose and His glory by His power and might, not yours. That means the pressure is off! You only have to follow where He leads you. He planned your purpose before you were ever conceived.

How can we doubt His purpose? How can we listen to the voices of those around us over the voice of the One who created us and formed us to do His work? How do we believe they know more about us than the One who made us? I assure you, dear brothers and sisters in Christ, no one knows you and knows the plans for you better than your heavenly Father. So, no matter what He's called you to do, step out in faith! Don't let the voices in your mind tell you more about your purpose than the One who created you.

Write About It: What are some things still hold you back from fulfilling God's purpose? What do you believe God's call is on your life?

Prayer: Dear Father, help me take the 't out of "can't" and make it "can." When the enemy tries to instill doubt, remind me of how You helped give courage to Your servant Jeremiah. Remind us that it's not what we can do but what You can do through us. We are Your servants, God; use us. Please show me what my purpose is, Amen.

Memory Verse: Jeremiah 1:5 - *Before I formed you in the womb, I knew you; before you were born, I sanctified you.*

Song Suggestion: "God of Purpose"- Metro Life Worship

Lie #11: I should be ashamed of myself after what I did.
Truth: In Christ, there is no shame.

Read: Romans 8:1-6

"You should be ashamed of yourself." Most of us have heard this phrase at one time or another. This phrase sounds biblical, but it's not. Biblical conviction doesn't look anything like shame. Conviction says, "You made a mistake." Shame says, "You are a mistake." Do you see the difference? Conviction says, "I've done something wrong and need to go to God for forgiveness of my sins." Shame says, "I should not exist, and I need to be gone."

When my PTSD was at its worst, I made mistakes that deeply affected not only myself but my husband, kids, and community. I was so ashamed of my mistakes, and it didn't help that others around me wouldn't let me forget them. It wasn't until I got involved with my current church that I learned how to hand those mistakes over to God. I learned to trust God with my history and what He wants to do with it instead of being ashamed of myself.

We are reminded in Romans 8 that if we are in Christ, we are not condemned. We walk with Jesus, no longer walking according to worldly desires, and are made free. We are not made guilty; we are not made shameful; we are not made broken; we are made free! Free from what? Free from sin and death! We no longer walk in sin, death, and shame. We walk in freedom with Jesus. The word free used here literally means to be set free!

Write About It: On a scrap piece of paper, make a list of things you are ashamed of and then destroy it. In destroying it, you are choosing to let those things be at the foot of the cross. Do you believe that God has forgiven you and made you new?

Prayer: Dear Father, we have worn the weight of shame for way too long, and we thank You for releasing us of our shame. We acknowledge that we don't deserve this release but that Your son, Jesus, gave it to us freely. Father, remind us daily that we are not condemned, broken or shameful. In Jesus' Name, we pray, Amen.

Memory Verse: Romans 8:1a - *There is, therefore, no condemnation to those who are in Christ Jesus.*

Song Suggestion: "Look What You've Done" - Tasha Layton

Lie #12: I'm dirty, used, and uncleaned. Truth: Jesus makes us clean.

Read: Luke 7:36-50

If you have PTSD from sexual abuse, feeling dirty, used, or uncleaned can be overwhelming. Although I'm sharing about a passage in which Jesus forgives a woman caught up in sexual sin, please know that sexual abuse is a sin committed against you and not a sin you committed. I'm sharing this passage because Christians hold on to sexual purity so badly that we often forget that Jesus handles sexual sin the same as any other sin. He forgives it and makes us new. Don't get me wrong, sexual purity is important, but it's important to know that those sins, whether you committed them or someone committed them against you, are forgiven. So, let's take a deeper look.

First, it's important to note that Jesus was at the house of a Pharisee. In today's world, they are known as holier-than-thou people. So, He's eating at some holier-than-thou person's home when one of "those women" walks in. This woman then poured oil on His feet, wiped them with her hair and tears, and even kissed His feet. The Pharisee was appalled that Jesus would even allow someone caught up in such sin to touch Him. Not only did Jesus allow her to interact with Himself, but after Jesus explained to the Pharisee why He was dead wrong, He told the woman, "Your sins are forgiven; go in peace." He didn't expect anything from her other than to stop doing what she was doing. She was told she was forgiven and could go in peace. Jesus didn't give her a lecture or make her confess to the people around Him; Jesus forgave her and made her clean! In fact, the person who got the lecture was the one who looked down on her.

Whether you feel unclean from a sin committed against you, a sin you committed, or both, know that Jesus is saying to you, "Go in peace." Not disgust or shame, but peace. Jesus has come to make you clean. You are unique to Him, and He loves you. He doesn't see you for what you've done or what was done to you. Instead, he sees you as a promised child of God, for whom He sacrificed Himself so that you would be made clean.

Write About It: What are some ways that you feel unclean? What does Jesus say about you?

Prayer: Oh, Father, this prayer is probably one of the hardest prayers because it causes me to go to a place I don't like. However, I need to go to that place, and I need You to go with me for true healing to happen. God, remind me that whatever happened to me or what I did, You have washed me and made me whiter than snow, and my shame is gone. Thank You, God, in Your Name, we pray, Amen.

Memory Verse: Luke 7:50 - *Then He said to the woman, "Your faith has saved you. Go in peace."*

Song Suggestion: "Something Has to Break"- Kierra Sheard, "Pour My Love On You" - Phillips Craig & Dean

Lie #13: There's no life left in me.
Truth: Jesus gives us life.

Read: John 11:38-44

There have been times in my life when I have felt lifeless. I seemed fine to most people, and the few that did notice thought the issue was that I wasn't "Trusting God enough." Although it was true, I hadn't completely trusted my life and entirety to Him; I was fighting brain-related impairments and PTSD that was so severe that I felt I couldn't get out of bed, and I dragged myself to complete every single task during the day. At night I relived the abuse in nightmares; it was so bad that I woke up feeling like the abuse from years ago had just happened. I felt so dead inside. I wasn't the wife or mother I wanted to be, and I thought of suicide often. Thankfully by God's grace, not only did I never attempt suicide, but I found new life in Jesus Christ.

In today's passage, we read the account of Jesus rising Lazarus from the dead. When Jesus went to Lazarus' tomb with Lazarus' sister Martha, Martha was doubtful that Jesus could do anything for him since he was in the tomb for four days. She even said he probably stinks. But Jesus said to her, "Did I not say that if you believe, you would see the glory of God?" Once the people who were gathered around with them took the stone away, Jesus lifted His eyes up and thanked God, and said, " I know you always hear me, but because of the people around me, I say this that they may believe that you sent me." Then He loudly cried out, "Lazarus come forth!" Amazingly, Lazarus came out of the tomb ALIVE but still wrapped in cloth from where he was laid in the tomb. Then Jesus said to them, "lose him and let him go."

Notice here that Jesus not only brought Lazarus back to life, but Jesus also commanded that his grave clothes be removed from him. Jesus not only wants to give you new life in Him, but He also wants to do it completely. He wants you to remove your grave clothes, the things you hold on to that are still a part of the dark tomb, He wants those, too! Not only do you need to believe He can bring you new life, but you also need to believe He can help you remove your grave clothes.

Write About It: What are some ways that you feel dead inside? What are some things that bring you life?

Prayer: Father, I thank You for still performing miracles in the 21st century. I believe You will bring me new life, remove my grave clothes. When that stone is rolled away, and I walk out of the tomb that I let the devil put me in, the devil will cry out, "Oh no!" I thank You, Jesus! Amen.

Memory Verse: John 11:40 - *Jesus said to her, "Did I not say to you that if you believe, you would see the glory of God?"*

Song Suggestion: "Raise Up (Lazarus)"- Cain

Lie #14: My well is too deep.
Truth: Your well isn't too deep for Jesus.

Read: John 4:12-26

The first public event I went to after the COVID shutdown ended was a small night of worship hosted by a ladies' group. During our worship time, one of the leaders went up to the mic and read the passage about the woman at the well. I heard the Holy Spirit speak to me and say, "Your well isn't too deep for me." I thought, "That's odd. The scripture really isn't about—" then the leaders shared what Jesus said about the woman having had five husbands, and then said, "Well... that tells us how deep her well was." Then I heard the Holy Spirit say again, "You're well isn't too deep for me."

During this time, I felt used, broken, lost, and so far away from God. I had just completely turned my life over to Him and trusted Jesus as my Savior during the pandemic but so much happened and came to light about my abuse as a child. As I remembered more of my childhood, I felt more and more lost. Everything in my life was a mess; my well was so deep. When Jesus met the woman at the well, he met her when she was broken, lost, and living an ungodly lifestyle, yet Jesus went to her. Jesus told her He was the living water, and through Him, she would thirst no more. He told her all the things she ever did and told her the hour had come when the worshippers would worship in spirit and in truth. She said to Him, "I know the Messiah is coming." And Jesus replied, "I am He." The woman left and told people in the city; many came to believe because she shared what Jesus said.

Her well wasn't too deep to be used by God. Whatever well or hole you're in, whether you fell in, were pushed in, or dug it yourself;

God is there. He knows all you've done, yet He sees you for what you can do through Him for His glory.

Write About It: What does your “well” look like? How can Jesus help you with your “well”?

Prayer: Father, thank You for reaching out Your hand and pulling me out of where I was. Use me, Lord, to advance Your kingdom. Use my past as a testimony to encourage others of how You rescued me from my hole. I praise You, God, for Your mercy and compassion. In Jesus' Name, Amen.

Memory Verse: John 4:26 - *Jesus said to her, "I who speak to you am He."*

Song Suggestions: “God Turn it Around” - Jon Reddick with Matt Maur, “Daughter of the King”- Yvonne Marie

Lie#15: I can't move on from what I've done. Truth: There is no sin too great God can't turn around for His glory.

Read: Acts 9:1-6, 9:20-22

Lives filled with trauma and PTSD often lead to more trauma and poor choices; for example, choosing a lifestyle of drugs and sex. Although I didn't fall into these traps, I fell into others. Codependency, perfectionism, debt, relationship issues, overthinking and needing to have control were my issues. These issues stem from trauma and various brain-related injuries. One day while conversing with my eldest daughter, I told her I was sorry our life wasn't normal. "Normal! God never used normal people in the Bible! I don't want to be normal, I want to be used by God! I believe God is going to use your struggles to do great things in your life and mine!" She was ten years old when this conversation took place, and she was, at that moment, wiser than I was. I had to decide to let God use my past mistakes, failures, and trauma instead of believing I couldn't move on.

In today's passage, Saul was met by the voice of the Lord while actively plotting to kill those who believed in Jesus. He was a murderer against God's people. After being stopped on the road and receiving instruction from the Lord, he went to the city and followed the Lord's instructions; thus, he converted to believing in Jesus. What happened after he was converted? He immediately began to preach the gospel in the synagogues. He grew spiritually and became the church's greatest advocate! What if Saul said, "I've murdered people. God can't use me! Why would anyone listen to me after what I've done?" Satan wants us to believe we can't move on from what we've done because he knows that when we do move on, we will become advocates and sharers of the life-saving truth of Jesus Christ.

Write About It: What are some things you did that you still hold on to? What are some ways that you can begin to hand those things over to God?

Prayer: Father, release me from this lie that I can't be used by You because of my past. Like Saul, I have been blind, but through Your grace and transformative power, I believe that you will not only restore my sight but also give me a new name and send me out to share your Word. Thank You, Father! Amen.

Memory Verse: Acts 9:22 - *But Saul increased all the more in strength and confounded the Jews who dwelt in Damascus, proving that this Jesus is the Christ*

Song Suggestions: "One Step Away"- Casting Crowns, "Erase" - Disciple

Lie #16: I need to get myself together.
Truth: We go to Jesus as we are, and He transforms us.

Read: Luke 5: 27-32

I used to believe this ridiculous idea that I had to "get myself together" and THEN present myself to Jesus. Sadly, I learned this idea in church. It's not deliberate teaching; it's something that develops from being told you need to act or dress a certain way at church. Don't go to church broken and falling apart; come dressed well and with excellent behavior. The Christian culture tells us to get ourselves together, become Christians then come to church. However, this idea is not only unbiblical, but it also just doesn't work to bring people to Christ.

In today's passage, we read about Matthew, also known as Levi, who was a tax collector. It's important to know that since he was a Jew and the Romans persecuted the Jews, it was an act of betrayal for him to work for the Romans as a tax collector. Tax collectors were also known for cheating the system by keeping money for themselves. Therefore, Matthew was an enemy to both the Jews and the Romans, a complete outcast, that is, until Jesus. Jesus walks up to Matthew at the tax office and says, "Follow me." Now I imagine that those who were around probably thought? "Does Jesus know whom He is talking to? Matthew the betrayer!" But Jesus saw who Matthew could be, so He asked Matthew to follow Him. He didn't say anything about who Matthew was. He didn't tell Mathew to get himself together first; Jesus simply said, "Follow me." Matthew then stopped everything He was doing, left everything behind, and followed Jesus.

The same is true for us. Jesus comes to us in the middle of our insanity and says, "Follow me." No other request is made of us. Do we change our hearts, minds, and actions over time? Yes, but we don't change ourselves; Jesus changes us. Therefore, we must first answer the command, "Follow me."

Write About It: What are some ways you've tried to change yourself instead of going to Jesus for the change and healing?

Prayer: Father, thank You for how You made me. Thank You for sending Jesus to die for me so I can be healed and changed for You. Forgive me for trying to change myself instead of going to You for healing. So help me, Father God, to go to You and only You for healing and change, Amen.

Memory Verse: Luke 5:27b-28 - *And He said, "Follow me." So he left all, rose up, and followed Him.*

Song Suggestion: "Different"- Micah Tyler

Lie #17: I'm destined to repeat the mistakes and sins of my family.
Truth: God will do a new thing in your life.

Read: Isaiah 43:18-21

One of the biggest lies I ever believed was that I was destined to repeat the mistakes and sins of my family. I got so distracted by the world, statistics, and what others around me were saying. Things like "You are just like them" and "Abused kids grow up and abuse their kids." Man, did I believe it! However, instead of turning around and giving that to God, I became overly focused on trying to prove to everybody that I was different. The problem was that by doing it in my own strength, I started repeating my biological family's mistakes. I remember crying out to God while listening to music, and I kept asking God, "Will I end up like them? Will my kids have a better life than I did? Am I stuck carrying down to my kids what happened to me?" God answered me in a song, "It's your sad reality, it's your messed up family tree, and now you're left with all these questions... Are you going to be like your father was... Do you have to carry down what they've handed down? No! This is not your legacy; this is not your destiny... I can break the chains that bind you." Hearing that song and those words, I fell on my knees and prayed for God to lead me and guide me. I would like to say that everything changed then and there, but it would take five more years for me to learn how to trust God with that and let go of my fear.

In this passage of Isaiah, Judah was being called to let go of the struggles they faced and be a nation among nations. They were being called to look away from the past and focus on the new destiny God had in store for them. Isaiah told them that God would make rivers in the desert and a road in the wilderness. God will make rivers in your desert and roads in your wilderness. First, you must let go of what was and choose not to linger on it. Instead, focus on God's destiny for you! Believe that God can! You are more than a statistic; you are His chosen. Be set free and declare His praise!

Write About It: What are the things in your family tree you are afraid of repeating? What are the things you are hoping for in your future?

Prayer: Lord, I turn these things over to You! In Your name, things are made new! My brokenness is made new! I am not stuck repeating the sins of our family because YOU made me. Yours!

Memory Verse: Isaiah 43:19a - *Behold, I will do a new thing.*

Song Suggestion: "Family Tree"- Matthew West

Lie #18: I'm not as good as ----.
Truth: It's not about how good YOU are, but how good He is.

Read: Ephesians 2:1-10

When you struggle with PTSD and other mental health issues, fighting off the need to compare yourself to "normal" people can be challenging. It's easy to look at the lives of others around you and think, " Boy, they sure have it together," or "I'm not as good as---because---" or "If only I didn't---." The lie that you are messed up and everyone else around you is all put together is a trap to keep you down in the pit instead of living for Jesus. This passage in Ephesians tells us that apart from Christ, we are nothing. We are dead, walking on earth in disobedience to God. It is only by our faith in Jesus that we are worth anything. It isn't because of anything we did or could do. It was a gift from God!

Remember, you are created in Christ for great things. He has a plan for your life. You are a workmanship of Christ! The word workmanship used in verse ten means "to make," as in art or pottery. Therefore, you are a masterpiece created by God, His greatest artwork! In the art world, a masterpiece cannot be copied. You are one-of-a-kind, designed by God to do His good works. His plan for you and your walk with Him will not match someone else's. So, don't get caught up focusing on others but on your walk with God and the plans He has for you.

Write About It: Do you have a person that you usually compare yourself to? Is there someone in your life that you look at and go, "Wow, they've got it all together?"

Prayer: Lord, thank You for making me who I am. Thank you for molding me to be more like You. Forgive me when I have compared myself to others. Help me to focus on You and how You see me, Amen.

Memory Verse: Ephesians 2:10 - *For we are His workmanship, created in Christ for good work, which God prepared beforehand that we should walk in them.*

Song Suggestion: "You Say"- Lauren Daigle

Lie#19: I need to prove my value.
Truth: You don't need to prove yourself to anyone.

Read: Matthew 4:5-11

I question my value—all the time. Unfortunately, for those of us recovering from PTSD stemming from abuse, this is all too common. We've been called stupid, fat, ugly, worthless, a failure, and words that do not fit the Christian tongue. As a result, we tend to question our value, not just who we are but WHOSE we are. I find myself doubting my value lately, between my past childhood abuse and people misjudging the situation I'm currently in. I find myself fighting heavy discouraging words. I find it worse now that I'm obeying God's call to write this book and start a ministry. I find myself tempted to focus on proving myself to others instead of on God's plan and will for my life. But do you know what I discovered? Jesus faced the same temptation.

After Jesus was baptized and before He started His ministry, He was tempted by Satan. During the time He was tempted, Satan took Him up to the top of the temple and said, "If you are the Son of God, throw yourself down for it is written, He shall give angels charge over you…." Matthew 4:5-6a. So, in other words, Satan takes Jesus up to the top of the temple and says prove it! Prove you are whom you say you are! If you really are the Son of God, then the angels will rescue you. But Jesus didn't need to prove His worth. He knew God's plans for Him and was confident in who He was and whose He was, God's Son. He knew God's plan, and it was not yet time for miracles. Jesus knew that "proving" who He was would not only have been tempting God but also it would have been stepping out of God's will and plan for His life.

Satan wants you to feel like you have to prove your value. Satan wants you to question who you are and that you are God's! He wants you to doubt your value in Christ because he wants you to be distracted with proving your value instead of following God's will for your life. So don't lose heart, and don't lose focus! Don't worry about proving your value. Rather, be confident in who you are! God's child

Write About It: What do you do to prove your value to yourself and others?

Prayer: Lord, help me to focus on You and Your plans for me. Please help me to be confident that I am Yours and not focus on what others think of me.

Memory Verse: Matthew 4:10 – *Jesus said to him, "Away with you, Satan! For it is written, you shall worship the Lord your God, and Him only you shall serve."*

Song Suggestion: "Confidence"- Sanctus Real

Lie #20: I need to hide my issues.
Truth: We need to share our struggles with people we trust.

Read: Galatians 6:1-3

Past experiences taught me that I was better off keeping my problems to myself. Over the years, I was overly judged and hurt by those who should have helped me the most. Because of this, I decided it was better to hide who I was and my issues. I certainly couldn't mention my abuse history and PTSD. Thankfully, God has placed a wonderful church and trusted people in my life. He is using my issues and PTSD to help others. This book, of course, is one example of how God is using my past to touch the lives of others; this is how it should be. Unfortunately, the church society is a significant culprit in hiding your brokenness and issues. The idea that church is where we wear our best clothes, act like we've got it all together, listen to some songs and a sermon, leave the building, and then not see or talk to anyone until next Sunday is not how it should be. Don't get me wrong, everyone doesn't need to know everything about us, but we shouldn't go to church acting like everything is fine when it isn't. The church is supposed to be a body of believers that come together like a family to be there for each other and support each other. Finding trusted believers to share your life with, especially the brokenness and issues you may be struggling with, is crucial. We need spiritually equipped individuals to help guide us gently in PTSD recovery as we heal and sometimes make mistakes.

Today's passage tells us that the spiritually fit should restore us to Christ with gentleness. It also says that we are to bear each other's burdens. It doesn't say we should hide things from each other, handle things ourselves, and act all "godly." It also says that if anyone thinks highly of themselves, they are deceiving themselves. Therefore, don't think so highly of yourselves that you think you can "handle it" on your own. That way of thinking is a trap laid by the enemy, and, in most situations, it will leave you unsuccessful. However, when we bare each other's burdens, we are doing what? It says that we are fulfilling the law of Christ. An example of the law of Christ would be to love your neighbor as yourself. When we support each other and guide each other through life's most challenging times, like trauma, for example, we are like Christ. So not only does sharing your issues make it more likely that you will be more successful, but it also makes you MORE like Christ.

Write About It: Write a short list of people you can visit for support for your PTSD recovery. Ask God to reveal these people to you.

Prayer: Lord, today, show me the people in my life that I can trust with my PTSD recovery. Lord, thank You for putting these people in my life. Lord, I'm sorry for thinking that I could do this alone. Show me how to share my battle cautiously but openly with those I trust, Amen.

Memory Verse: Galatians 6:2 - *Bear one another's burdens, and so fulfill the law of Christ.*

Song Suggestion: "Stained Glass Masquerade"- Casting Crowns

Lie #21: I can't move on from what happened.
Truth: With time, you can move on.

Read: Philippians 3:12-16

Once I got past the flashbacks and trauma responses, once I learned how to manage my PTSD symptoms, and once I learned ways to cope with all the memories, I still had the heartbreak to heal from. I had to choose to let go of the heartbreak and give that to God, too. I had to decide not to linger on the past and "what if's" or what could have been.

In Philippians, Paul talks about pressing on and forgetting things behind him, pressing toward the call of God in Jesus Christ. He isn't talking about forgetting, as in just pressing a delete button and deleting the memory of what happened or who hurt you. Paul is telling us not to linger on the past but instead press forward. You may feel like you can never move past what happened or move past your broken heart, but over time, if you keep focusing on the race set before you and allowing Jesus to heal you, the memories will fade, and your heart will begin to heal.

Write About It: List some ways you still hang on to what happened to you. How can you choose to let go of those things and surrender them to Jesus Christ?

Prayer: Lord, today, I give You my past, trauma, and heartbreak. I pray, Father God, that You might help me to look to You and what You have set before me instead of what is behind. Thank You for being my Healer. Amen.

Memory Verse: Philippians 3:13 - *Brethren, I do not count myself to have apprehended; but one thing I do, forgetting those things which are behind and reaching forward to those things which are ahead.*

Song Suggestion: "Haven't Seen it Yet"- Danny Gokey

Lie #22: IF God loved me, He wouldn't have let---- happen.
Truth: God has a plan, even if you don't see it.

Read: Esther 4:1-17

In May 2019, two men lost their battle with cancer. One gentleman I loved like a brother, and the other gentleman was the brother-in-law of a close friend of mine. Both men were fathers of small children. One had two little boys, and the other had six kids. They died within hours of each other. My daughter had dental surgery that day, so I kept a brave face for her, but when we got home, and she was asleep, all that pent-up anger turned into a foot size hole in my hallway wall! This was something I'd never done before or since. But at that moment, I don't think I've ever been angrier at God. Even with my past abuse, this cut me deeper. During that time, I remember going for a drive and singing along to the radio, "You are good, You are good, ooooh." As I was singing, the Holy Spirit started talking to me, and I said, "I believe You are good; I just don't understand why this has happened to them." Then I realized that even in things I don't understand, I know He is always good. I knew this was true even when I didn't see what or why He was good.

Before Esther was Queen Esther, she was Hadassa. She was orphaned and raised by her cousin Mordecai. The king chose her to be his queen even though she had no desire to be his queen. As a matter of fact, at that time, a number of Jews were still in Babylon under Persian rule. A man named Hayman, the king's right-hand man, planned to have every Jew killed. So for Esther, being in the palace was very dangerous because she was a Jew. Mordecai sent a message to Esther and asked her to speak to the king on behalf of her people.

But Esther was afraid. Mordecai questioned her, "What if God has put you there for such a time as this?" God used Esther to save her people from being killed, and God spared Esther's life.

What about you? Do you feel like God is not there? He is there. Even though the name of God is not mentioned in the book of Esther, His fingerprints and proof of His handiwork are everywhere. Even if you are in a place where you can't even speak His name, He is there. Esther was put in a place she didn't want to be, but God used her position to save her people. Esther got to see some of the reasons God had put her there, but some of us don't get to see the "why" in this lifetime. Even if you don't see it, even if you can't see it right now, God has you right where He wants you for a reason. It's not that He doesn't care about what's happening, and it's not that He doesn't love you, you just can't always see the "why." Remember, God is greater than us, and even in the darkest times, He's holding on to you, and He is still good.

Write About It: Do you feel God in your struggles? How can He use your struggles to help others? What are some things that you still hold on to?

Prayer: Lord, help me to trust You even when things seem like they are falling apart. Help me see it's in those times things are being carefully put in place by You. Lord, I trust that you make all things come together for my good. Amen

Memory Verse: Esther 4:14b -*"Yet, who knows whether you have come to the kingdom for such a time as this?"*

Song Suggestions: "King of My Heart"- Kutless, "Held" - Casting Crowns

Lie #23: I don't need to forgive my abuser. Truth: We need to forgive even the most harmful act.

Ephesians 4:31-32

Paul's words of setting aside bitterness and forgiving one another sound like an excellent Sunday school lesson until we talk about forgiving murderers, rapists, and child molesters. Not those people. Sure, we can forgive the guy who dinged our car or our child for coloring on the walls, but when it comes to "those people," we tend to put on the breaks. "Oh, but God doesn't mean them." Yes, my friend, He means them, too. No, God doesn't tell you that you have to invite unsafe people over for dinner who refuse to come to repentance for what they have done. However, true forgiveness and setting aside bitterness is something I've learned that leads to healing.

I want to share something with you that I initially believed should not be shared in the public setting of this book. However, I find it difficult to talk about forgiveness without sharing this, and I believe the testimony I'm about to share is so important.

I had flashbacks as a teenager and young adult. Because of the things that ran through my mind during the flashbacks, I was afraid to tell anyone about them. It wasn't until 2019 that I finally started to deal with it. Over time, as people began to disclose things they heard and saw and my memories became clearer, I began to remember more of the sexual abuse I experienced as a 2-4-year-old child. Unfortunately, by the summer of 2020, we discovered that the physical issue I had been struggling with since I was a child was most likely caused by childhood abuse.

I tell you that to tell you this: God has taught me a lot about forgiveness. We must remember that Jesus died for even the barbarians of this world. Jesus died even for those who would force a child to do something so heinous at such a young age. Forgiveness is not just praying for my abuser but praying he will one day know Jesus as I do. This means I will welcome him as a brother in Christ whom I might worship with in heaven someday. That's what true forgiveness is. Forgiveness isn't just saying, "Yeah, Jesus died for him, too." Forgiveness is worshiping Jesus BECAUSE He died for him, too. Forgiveness is celebrating that Jesus died and that I'm no more deserving of God's favor, grace, mercy, and forgiveness than my abuser. Accepting these truths will be hard at first, but it will lead you to complete and total healing.

Write About It: Is there someone that you still need to forgive? If so, who? Is it hard or easy for you to forgive them? What do you think about God sending His only son, Jesus, to die for us so that we could be forgiven while we were still His enemies?

Prayer: Lord, thank You for sending Your son to die on the cross to forgive our sins. Jesus, I ask You to teach me how to forgive even the hardest offenses. You know how I feel because you were also betrayed. Help my heart to be more like Yours, Amen.

Memory Verse: Ephesians 4:32b - *...forgiving one another, even as God in Christ forgave you.*

Song Suggestion: "Forgiveness"- Matthew West

Truth Point#1: God wants every last bit of us, even the trash.

By: Whitfield-Pogue

*This was written but a leader in the women's ministry at my church for an event. Used with permission. *

I have an infatuation with lotion. I love the smell, the texture, and the way it feels when it glides across my skin. I know it sounds silly, but it just makes me happy. It doesn't matter if it is expensive or inexpensive; I love all sorts of lotions, creams, and moisturizers. I line them up on my bathroom counter just to admire the pretty containers and as a reminder to use them. I stash lotion in my car, purse, and office. If I see someone else using lotion, I've even been known to ask for a bit for myself.

When the lotion container is getting low, I will squeeze it, bang on it, and contort it in all sorts of directions in an attempt to get every last drop out of the tube. I will whittle away at the tube, cutting it into sections until I can successfully dig, swipe, and glean every bit trapped on the sides and in the corners. To me, the lotion is like precious oil. I can't bear to part with it until I have fully exhausted it.

This is the way that Jesus wants us to come to Him. He wants us to whittle away at ourselves and dig, swipe, and glean all that we can from Him and His Word. I actually dug this last tube out of my trash can to keep as an example. Although that was a bit of a humbling exercise for me, I felt the Lord impress upon me to share that even if all you have to bring Him is your trash, having fully exhausted all other avenues, this is precisely the way He wants you to come to Him.

Truth Point #2: Your identity is in the One who created you.

By: Mark Wynn

True story, around 2018 BC (Before Covid), I went to the funeral of an elderly lady that I took care of. When her daughter introduced me to the family, she DIDN'T say, "Hey everyone, meet Mark, a respectable CNA who took excellent care of my mother. Instead, believe it or not, she turned to the family and said, "This is Mark. He's the man who took mother to the bathroom." Right away, the identity given to me was that of a butt wiper.

In the world, we often use our job titles to identify ourselves and others. The person's name and job occupation are usually brought up when someone is introduced to someone else. Imagine if we all just identified ourselves by how God sees us instead of our job titles. How would we be changed if we believed that we were a child of God and royalty instead of just a plumber, a CNA, or a stay-at-home mom? The Bible says in 1 Peter 2:9, "But you are a chosen generation, a royal priesthood, a holy nation, His own special people, that you may proclaim the praises of Him who called you out of darkness into His marvelous light" (emphasis added).

My wife, Tabytha, had abusive parents and was bullied at school. Her parents and peers called her ugly, unintelligent, and worthless. She has carried this into adulthood. If we get into an argument and I speak in a harsh tone toward her, she may compare this to an experience with her parents. This allows the enemy to whisper lies in her ear as the serpent did to Eve. The same thing is true for me. I was bullied in school and abused by my dad. My peers called me things like "dumb" and" brainless." So if my wife says I'm acting stupid, instead of considering my foolishness, I might start believing that I am stupid. In turn, I might shut down or become enraged with anger and fire insults at her. It wasn't until we got the help that we began to work on the underlining issue; misunderstanding our true identities.

The underlining issue is that we allowed the labels others had assigned to us to be our nametag. How foolish would it look if we worked at a store and our nametag said "stupid" or "worthless"? Instead, our nametag should say, "Hello, my name is Child of the One True King" (Thank you, Matthew West). If you are struggling with repressed PTSD and just starting this journey, it might take a little bit longer not to believe the lies ingrained in your brain. Psalm 139:14 says, "I will praise You, for I am fearfully and wonderfully made; Marvelous are Your works, and that my soul knows very well" (emphasis added). How is your identity going to change after reading this? Are you going to believe the serpent or the Creator that loves you?

Truth Point #3: You haven't failed till you give up.

As you are probably already aware, the symptoms of those of us recovering from trauma experience are described as post-traumatic stress disorder or PTSD. However, I believe post-traumatic stress injury, or PSI is more accurate. Perhaps even PTSR, R for recovery. Please understand this, if you have PTSD, you are recovering from a traumatic event. You have been injured. Something has happened to you. Something has happened to your life. Your brain, your spirit, your emotions, they've all been affected. Therefore, be kind to yourself, give yourself time to heal, and allow yourself the grace to make mistakes even if others around you don't understand why you struggle or even why you do some of the things you do. Understand me, this doesn't mean you get a "get out of jail free card." You must take responsibility for your actions. Nonetheless, knowing that you are recovering from an injury allows a more profound understanding that you need to allow yourself room for extra grace. Therefore, be kind to yourself and know that you will make mistakes and fail at times but please also understand you haven't indeed failed unless you have given up.

When you fail, it's easy to want to give up when you and others around you see you as a failure. It's easy to get caught up in what others think or say about you. This is especially true if you have suffered verbal abuse, such as being called stupid, useless, failure, etc. This type of abuse is something you carry into adulthood and can impact how you view yourself and cause you to primarily focus on the fact that you fell instead of focusing on God's plan for your life and how He can help you get back up. This was true for me. I really struggled with keeping my focus on God and getting back up. I labeled myself a failure and stayed down instead of rising up. However, by digging into the Word of God and replacing lies with His truth, I learned two things: other people's opinions about my struggles aren't what I should focus on, and God isn't so much concerned with my failures as He is my repentance.

Proverbs 24:16 says that even though a righteous man falls seven times, he still gets back up. See, God's emphasis is not on who fell down or even how long they stayed down but on whether or not they get back up. Take David, for example, he took a married woman as his own, and when she got pregnant, he tried to lie and manipulate the situation. When that didn't work, he committed murder. Yet, he was still considered a man after God's own heart because he turned back to God. Therefore, I encourage you. God knows you will fail. He knows you will backslide. He knows you will fall. God doesn't expect perfection, God simply asks that when you fall, you look up to Him for strength and, in His strength, get back up.

Truth Point #4: Fear is a liar.

I used to live in fear. As a child, I was afraid of making any mistakes or forgetting to do something that was asked of me. I carried this fear into adulthood but didn't know it was fear. It had other names codependency, perfectionism, insecurity, nightmares, etc. Fear is a liar! Fear will keep you stuck. Fear will tell you that you're not good enough. Fear will keep you from living out God's plan for your life.

Psalms 23;4 says, "...though I walk through the valley of the shadow of death, I will fear no evil." I love the use of the word "shadow" here. Shadows tend to give the appearance of something else. Like a tree casting what looks like a scary shadow of a ghost outside a child's bedroom window. If we are in Christ, death is not real, it's just a shadow. So, when we walk through the valley of the shadow of death, we fear no evil. Because death can't hurt us, it can only take us from earth into heaven with Jesus. Therefore, we don't fear death. Now, that doesn't mean we don't protect ourselves. God has us here for a reason, so we should do our best to keep ourselves safe. However, we don't need to live in fear of death.

A shadow also appears when an object blocks a light source. So don't let your past block Jesus' light in your life. In Him, we have nothing to fear! Psalms 27:1 says, "The Lord is my light and salvation; whom shall I fear?" His love and death on the cross cover all our fears. His light is all you need to feel safe. He loves you.

I remember when I was about 11, I was having a sleepover at the house of the family who would one day adopt me, and my now-adoptive dad came in to make sure my now-adoptive sister and myself were asleep. I pretended to be asleep as he entered the room, checked on us, and left and told my now adoptive mom in the other room, “Yep, they are out cold, tucked nice and snug.” That was the first time, and one of the only times I didn’t wet the bed as a child. It was because, at that moment, I had a father figure that made me feel safe. I felt safe and at peace, as if someone loved me. Actually, I felt safe and at peace BECAUSE I felt like someone loved me. According to I John 4:18, “perfect love casts out fear.” There is no love in fear. We can't both be consumed with Jesus’ love AND be afraid. So, consume yourself with Jesus by reading God's Word and praying. This is how we defeat fear. Although we need to trust in Jesus as our source of peace, trauma causes fear like no other, and it's not as simple as just waking up and deciding to trust Jesus; it takes time, prayer, Bible reading, therapy, and in some cases, medication. In your PTSD recovery, remember that Jesus is Immanuel, which means “God with us.” Matthew 28:20 says, “He is with us always!” That means He is with you in your fear and trauma, too.

Truth Point #5: Volunteering aids in your healing.

When I was 17, I started volunteering at a Christian ministry. They had a thrift store which they used to raise money. I became friends with the staff there; over time, they became like my family. They took me to their church, where I learned that I wasn't walking the walk of a Christ follower but of someone who was faking it. In this ministry, I learned that I needed healing. God used my volunteering experience to grow closer to Him, and it became a tool He would use to heal me. I met people who would later become my church family while I lived in Tennessee. I'm still in contact with the people at that church, and even though I live eight hours away from them, they are still my family. Now my husband and I go to a church in Maryland, and once again, He is using my time to volunteer to help heal me.

My church, where my family and I currently attend and call home, hosted a concert for Jeremy Camp. It was significant to me because I first chose to follow Jesus at a youth event, and he was one of the singers there. At this youth group retreat, I was carrying around a heavy darkness. So many times, I thought about killing myself. So many times, I thought the world was better off without me. Jeremy Camp's music and message were the tools God used to bring me back to Him. So when I found out that my church needed volunteers to help Jeremy Camp, I jumped at the chance. I didn't meet Jeremy Camp or anything like that, I just cleaned the bathrooms that morning, then unloaded heavy stuff out of a truck, set it up, tore it down, and reloaded it back onto a truck. And guess what? I never felt more blessed to do heavy lifting and scrub toilets because I could give back after what God used Jeremy Camp for in my life. It was an honor and privilege to give back to his ministry. It was an honor to work alongside some great volunteers knowing that the gospel message makes a difference. And just like at the youth group event when I was 17, much healing took place at this event. I made new friends, and I grew closer to my church family. There is just something powerful about what God does through volunteers. As I volunteered that day, I struggled again with hopelessness, but God brought back the memory of me as a 17-year-old girl and how far I had come. Volunteering at the concert and working alongside others helped me come out of my shell and open up to my church family. So even though I didn't get to fist pump Jeremy Camp or a selfie with him, I received much more.

Taking the time to step out of your own life and routine can make a difference during your recovery from PTSD. Taking the time to think of others can actually bring healing for yourself. Although you may feel stuck and think that now is not the time to volunteer, I encourage you to make time. Making the time to volunteer takes the focus off of yourself and can really make a difference in your recovery. Find someplace where you can give some of your time and energy, even if it's just one hour a week or even one hour a month.

Truth Point #6: Jesus' touch heals shame.

I had always felt an overwhelming sense of shame. Like a heavy weight on my back, I carried around all this shame I put on myself; shame from abuse, shame from mistakes I've made, and issues I now have in my life from making those mistakes. In the past, I have gone to God with this, knowing that He forgives ALL sins and even FORGETS them. ALL of them! But even still, I continued to carry this shame around every day until recently.

I was in a church Bible class and was challenged to memorize a passage from the book of Romans. After reading it over, I decided to memorize the verses before and after the passage because those words were powerful to my heart. Let's look at Romans 10:8-13. It starts by asking the question, "But what does it say?" Good question. What do the scriptures say? Let's keep going. "The word is near you in your mouth and in your heart." Notice it said the word is NEAR you, not far away, but near you. It's not in some faraway place somewhere but right where you are. Also, what word is it that's near you? Well, let's look... "That is the word of Faith which we preach, that if you confess with your mouth the Lord Jesus and believe on your heart that God has raised Him from the dead, you will be saved." Wow! So, the scripture says that the word of FAITH is near you and that if you confess and believe, you will be saved. Not the word of fear nor the word of worry nor is it the word of shame BUT the word of FAITH that SAVES you! It gets even better, so let's read on. "For with the heart one believes unto righteousness, and with the mouth, confession is made unto salvation. For the scripture says whoever believes in Him will not be put to shame. For there is no distinction between Jew and Greek, for the same Lord over all is rich to all who call upon Him. For whoever calls on the name of the Lord shall be saved." You are right with God because you believe in Jesus' death and resurrection, confessed your sins, and expressed out loud that Jesus is Lord. Did you catch the next part? You are not put to shame because you believe in Jesus. There is no difference between God's chosen people and those who hung him on the cross. There is no difference between someone that grew up in church and got saved at an early age and someone who was a drug dealer and didn't get saved until they were in their thirties. Memorizing that scripture enabled me to quote it every time the devil tried to put shame on me for something I've done or something that was done to me. I remember that everything is covered by the blood of Jesus and forgiven.

But my healing from shame didn't begin there; it started about four months ago while I was away on a ladies' retreat. There was a massage therapist there, she had great rates, and my friends encouraged me to try her out. But I just couldn't do it. Touch was still a very triggering thing for me, especially something like that! But as the Lord would have it, I ran into her at the buffet line, and we talked. The conversation ended with her saying, "It sounds like someone used touch to hurt you instead of love you. Touching, when done right, is loving and healing. It sounds like you need some healing touch." Well, I went to her signup sheet and signed up for her to give me a massage. To my surprise, it was the best experience ever. I didn't freak out, wasn't triggered, and had no panic attacks. I had been set free! At that same retreat, I got a butterfly print that said, "Set Free" with the reference of Galatians 5:1, which says, "Christ made us FREE." Therefore, we are not to be tangled up in bondage anymore! We are set free to be no longer held in captivity of our sin or shame that was put on us from abuse. The massage therapist was right; there's healing power in touch.

Jesus showed us how powerful and healing faith, hope, and one touch could be in our lives with the miracles He performed. My favorite example is the woman with the issue of blood in Mark 5:27-

32. She suffered isolation and lost all her money to physicians who couldn't find a cure for her bleeding. But she heard of Jesus and believed He could heal her even if all she could do was touch the hem of his garment. According to the biblical laws, it would have been unlawful for her to be in the crowd or to touch anyone because of her illness, much less someone who was considered a religious leader like Jesus. But she took a step of faith and touched the hem of his clothing, thinking no one would notice, but Jesus noticed her. He even asked the question, "Who touched me?" Isn't it interesting that He asked that question? He had to have known who touched Him because He was fully man and fully God. If He knew, why did He ask? Well, let's keep reading. According to Luke 8: 47-48, She was trembling, and only when she saw that she could no longer be hidden she went to Jesus, fell to His feet and declared the truth in front of all the people. Then Jesus said to her, "Daughter…" WOW! He called her DAUGHTER, not uncleaned, not unlawful, but DAUGHTER, and then He said, "be of good cheer, your faith has made you well, GO IN PEACE." Not go in fear, disgust, or shame but peace. So, in the midst of all her shame, in front of all those people, He calls her daughter and tells her to go in peace. I believe that's why He asked, "Who touched me?" so she couldn't just hide and sneak off, still hanging on to her shame. He didn't want to just heal her of her health issue, He wanted to heal her of her shame as well. He wanted to make her whole. He wanted her and those around to know that she was HIS daughter and that SHE belonged to Him.

Brothers and sisters in Christ, He wants to heal your shame. He healed mine and made me a brand-new creation. He can do the same for you; He can break through the chaos and madness of your PTSD, trauma, poor choices, or any other mental health issues. The best part is that you don't have to do anything; only ask Him. Close your eyes, reach out, and touch Him, and He will make you whole.

Truth Point #7: Not everything is your fault, and not everything is your trauma's fault.

By: Mark and Tabytha Wynn

A popular game show from 2002 was called Whammy! The All-New Press Your Luck! The main difference between this and the original show was the double whammies. When a contestant landed on a double whammy, they not only lost all their cash and prizes but also got flour, water, or whatnot dumped on them.

Discovering that I (Mark) was struggling with inner child issues and PTSD for the past 12+ years is like hitting the double whammy. The good news is that there is now a reason why I was acting out all those years. That doesn't mean I get a "get out of jail free" card for how I acted. The truth is that, ultimately, I'm responsible for my actions. I could go around and say, "I would apologize for cursing you out, but you triggered me, and I can't help it." However, it would be more Christ-like to say, "I recently discovered that I am struggling with some issues, but that does not excuse how I talked to you over the years, and I am here to ask for forgiveness." As I am writing this, I am just a few weeks into the discovery of my inner child recovery and PTSD recovery process, and it is a struggle at times not to want to blame my actions on my past trauma. I'm not going to lie to you. Therefore, it is important to have mentors, accountability partners, brothers and sisters in Christ, to help keep us from blaming our past for our present mistakes. I'm not dismissing that we will slip up because of how we used to be before we started the recovery process, but we need to run to the Father daily and ask for strength and wisdom to keep healing daily and become more like Him.

If we start unpacking the past, we'll get triggered and relapse. But if we recognize our triggers, with God's guidance, we can overcome. 2 Corinthians 5:17 says, "Therefore, if anyone is in Christ, he is a new creation; old things have passed away; behold, all things have become new." If we unpack our past in a healthy, supportive environment, with God leading the way, it will be much harder for us to relapse.

Although it is important to take responsibility for our actions, it is equally important that we don't over-blame ourselves. We must be careful not to take responsibility for things that aren't our fault; this is especially true for victims of abuse or sexual assault. Don't take on blame that doesn't belong to you. I (Tabytha) tend to get stuck in a cycle of thinking that I can't do anything right, so I don't bother doing anything, which leads people to get angry at me. In turn, I feel like I can't do anything right, and the cycle keeps going. It is equally important that you do not hold on to your past wrongdoings. Once you seek forgiveness and reconciliation with God and the people you've wronged, you are NO LONGER GUILTY.

Truth Point #8: The Victory is ours because the battle is His.

"We aren't remodeling the walls of Jericho. Did you hear me? We aren't remodeling the walls of Jericho." Those were the words a good friend said to me when I called her crying about the battle I was facing. She didn't explain what that meant, but the Holy Spirit did, and we just cried together. The walls weren't getting remodeled; they weren't going to get prettied up or hidden, they weren't going to be ignored or covered up. They were coming down. Joshua 5:13- 6:5 tells us about when an angel appeared to Joshua and said to him that God had given Jericho to his hands. The angel gave Joshua instructions on how the walls would come down; now, the angel didn't say the Lord will give Jericho into your hands or might give it; no, God's message was, "I HAVE given them to you! I have already won this battle for you! You don't need to fear because I went before you! Even though you can't see it, the walls have already fallen!"

I'm here to tell you today that God has already fought the battle for you, you just need to be faithful to God's instructions. The walls fell not only because HE WENT BEFORE Joshua but because Joshua obeyed God's instructions. Joshua 6:6-20 tells us that Joshua was faithful to follow God's instructions, and the walls did fall. Joshua and the Israelites had to choose to obey those crazy instructions to walk around the city walls. God didn't tell them to storm the walls with weapons. He gave them crazy instructions that didn't make sense, but Joshua followed them anyway. Guess what? He started following God's instructions right away. He didn't debate with the angel or argue what God had told him, he went and did what God asked. Therefore, brothers and sisters in Christ, we must follow God's instructions faithfully, and if they don't make sense at first, follow God anyway. Even if those around you (not speaking of Godly counsel) are judging and talking about you, do what God has called you to do anyway.

Speaking of doing what God's called you to do, I admire Nehemiah and his strength. He was called to lead the people of Jerusalem to rebuild the walls. He did not stop his work for anything. In Nehemiah chapter six, we read that Nehemiah's enemies were plotting against him. They tried to attack him by way of the people around him, and they tried to distract him with false accusations. When I faced similar situations, I became hyper-focused on what others were plotting or thinking. Not Nehemiah, he simply said I am doing a great work, and I cannot stop. He went right on working. He knew the importance of finishing the wall and trusted God's will in the situation. Nehemiah's response came from his trust in God; my response came from trauma. What about you? Are you in the battle responding based on trauma or based on trusting in God?

Truth Point #9: We need to trust after trauma.

This morning my husband and I stood in front of the church to become members. To say, "This is my church family." I struggle with the idea of "trusting a family." Most of my family experiences have been abusive or dysfunctional. I also struggle with making and keeping relationships. Worst of all, I have been hurt by pastors and people within the church community, even abused by a pastor. Because of my history, standing up on stage and committing to membership was a big deal. I was ready to run, I was afraid to be up there. I was afraid I would be hurt again as I have been in the past...overcome by so much fear. Fear is a lie (See truth point #4), and I knew it, but it didn't keep me from being afraid to trust the church as my family. Don't get me wrong, I have been a part of a church family and experienced Christ-centered worship with a church family in the past. We were going to a church where we were all family and led by the Spirit, but that church is now seven hours from where our family lives now. I hadn't experienced this feeling of being a part of a church family since we left, at least not until October 13th, 2021. I was ready to give up on church, but a friend talked me into visiting their church. So, on that ordinary day in October, we visited Gateway Church in Williamsport, Maryland. Mark and the kids liked it, so we kept coming back. Truth be told, I struggled to open up to people and let people into my world. This was not just because of past church experiences, not just from all the abuse and hurt, but also because I felt that people were better off not knowing me. I was afraid, broken, ashamed, distrusting, and alone. I was perfectly okay with keeping my head down and getting the most I could out of the church. Still, when it came to developing relationships, I couldn't have been happier to avoid people altogether. Let's just say that's not how it worked out. The people at the church have been some of the most loving people I've ever met. Sure, there will be issues, and we won't always agree, but I learned something from this church.... They love people, they love my family, and surprisingly, they love me.

Today was a strange day for me. I was afraid to stand up in front of the church and commit to being a member. My husband grabbed hold of me and told me, "Don't let the enemy steal this day." I went up on stage with the other new members, and the pastor told all of us how much he loved us, how we could go to him if we needed something and things about being new members. He went to each new member, welcoming them and then he came to my husband and me and hugged us. I was surprised at what happened next. He told us how he was proud of us and loved us, and guess what? I believed him. At that moment, when I chose to believe him, I realized that I had never truly believed the words "I love you" before. Sadly, not even when my husband told me. I can't think of a single time until that moment that I ever really trusted someone. Don't get me wrong, people will fail us; we are human, after all. We will make mistakes. There will be times when our mistakes hurt the people that love us. When I say I didn't trust people, I mean I didn't trust that they really loved me. I believed there would eventually be a day when they would take advantage of me or turn out to be predators or some sort of evil-doers. I also thought about how hard it's been for me even to trust that God loves me.

How can we be followers of Christ if we don't love other people or trust other people to love us? How can we follow Christ if we doubt His love for us? The simple answer is that we can't. God did not design us to be alone. We were not designed to do life without Him, and we weren't designed to do life without each other. We need each other. We need other people in our lives to help us grow closer to God and encourage one another. Although there are cautions in the Bible about when and how to trust people, don't believe the lie from the enemy that you don't need people. Proverbs 27:17 says, "As iron sharpens iron, so a man sharpens the countenance of his friend." John 13:34-35 says, "A new commandment I give to you, that you love one another; as I have loved you, that you also love one another. By this, all will know that you are my disciples if you have a love for one another." It doesn't say we can hide from each other and do our own thing. We are commanded to love as Jesus loved. Jesus didn't hide away from people, and He didn't keep himself from making relationships. Jesus loved by making relationships with His disciples and others in the communities where He lived or visited. He did so by sharing God's Word, meeting people where they were in their brokenness or sickness, eating with those who were considered the scum of the earth, and even washing the feet of the very person who would betray Him.

Therefore, despite what our history is or what our struggles are, we are called to make relationships with the body of Christ. Even if you have tried twenty churches, keep trying until you find the right one. I almost gave up on church and people, and I'm glad I didn't. Don't let the enemy use your past experiences or even your faults to keep you from what God has in store for you; a body of Christ to call family. Not a perfect family, but a family you can trust to walk alongside you as you grow in Christ. Today, I choose to trust in the Lord with all my heart instead of leaning on my own understanding based on past experiences (Proverbs 3:5). Today, August 14th, 2022, I laid down the chains of fear and chose to trust.

Closing Thoughts

I pray this book has been helpful to your healing and growth as you set out to conquer PTSD. I hope you will keep looking back on this book and, more importantly, the Bible as your journey continues. Moving forward, you will have bad days where you might feel like giving up, but I pray that you put your faith and trust in Jesus Christ, not only as your Lord and Savior but as your Healer. Please know that I pray for God to touch the hearts and lives of anyone who reads this book. I hope this book will draw you closer to God as you heal. As you continue to heal, cry out to Him. I know that He hears you and is with you. He is walking with you or carrying you, always.

John 16:33(NLT)

"I have told you all this so that you may have peace in me. Here on earth, you will have many trials and sorrows. But take heart because I have overcome the world."

Resources

For a Free Bible, go to: wordfm.org/request-a-free-bible

For Men who struggle with sexual addiction linked to PTSD:
innerchild-sexaddiction.com/

To find a local Celebrate Recovery ® group go to:
locator.crgroups.info/

Looking for a website that connects women with God and each other? Check out: connectingwomenwithgod.com/

Looking for a website that connects men with God and each other? Check out: www.dadtired.com/

For free Christ-centered resources to help you heal from trauma, check out: traumahealingbasics.org/

Made in the USA
Middletown, DE
23 February 2023

25414314R00050